© Copyright YGM – All rights reserved. The content contained within this book may not be reproduced, duplicated or transmitted without direct written permission from the author or the publisher. Under no circumstances will any blame or legal responsibility be held against the publisher, or author, for any damages, reparation, or monetary loss due to the information contained within this book. Either directly or indirectly.

You are responsible for your own choices, actions, and results. Legal Notice: This book is copyright protected. This book is only for personal use. You cannot amend, distribute, sell, use, quote, or paraphrase any part, or the content within this book, without the consent of the author or publisher. Disclaimer

Notice: Please note the information contained within this document is for educational and entertainment purposes only. All effort has been executed to present accurate, up-to-date, and reliable, complete information. No warranties of any kind are declared or implied. Readers acknowledge that the author is not engaging in the rendering of legal, financial, medical, or professional advice.

The content within this book has been derived from various sources. Please consult a licensed professional before attempting any techniques outlined in this book. By reading this document, the reader agrees that under no circumstances is the author responsible for any losses, direct or indirect, which are incurred as a result of the use of the information contained within this document, including, but not limited to, — errors, omissions, or inaccuracies

WHAT IS SELF-TALK?

I can't wait for today

When you have conversations in your
head this is seen as
SELF-TALK

As you know, you are always having conversations in your head.

'I wonder what I am going to have to dinner'

'I can't wait for school today'

'I love this movie'

These are all normal thoughts which we have every day.

Some thoughts that we have in a day can be controlled by what's happening in our outside world

FOR EXAMPLE

You start skipping with your friends if you really good then you might think.

'WOW I love skipping'

'I'm so good at this game'

Positive self-talk

'WOW I love skipping'
'I am so good at this game'

This is seen as
POSITVE SELF-TALK

But if say you started playing the guitar and you weren't good you might have thoughts like

'Why am I so bad at this'

'I hate playing the guitar this is rubbish'

Negative self-talk

'Why am I so bad at this'
'I hate playing the guitar this is rubbish'

This is seen as
NEGATIVE SELF-TALK

Why is self-talk so important?

The conversations we have in our head about ourselves, shape our beliefs and have the power to influence our emotions and the way we behave

LET COMPARE THE USES OF POSITIVE SELF-TALK

- It makes you feel sure of yourself
- It makes you feel motivated
- It can help you make better decisions
- It makes you feel good about yourself
- It makes you feel happy about the future
- It makes you look forward to challenges

RISKS OF NETAGIVE-SELFTALK

- It makes you feel bad about yourself

- It can make you have a negative outlook

- It can make you feel more stressed

- It leads to you feel less motivated

- Makes you feel scared of challenges

DIFFERNET TYPES OF NETAGIVE-SELFTALK

Personalising

This is when you blame yourself for all the bad things in your life.

'This is all my fault'

'I am so stupid, why did I do that'

DIFFERNET TYPES OF NETAGIVE-SELFTALK

FILTERING

This is when you focus only on the negative information and ignore the positive. This can leave you feeling helpless.

Traing your self talk to be more positive and optimistic

Thankfully you can train self talk to be more positive by practicing the techniques you're about to learn.

HERE ARE 3 DIFFERENT TEACHNIQUES YOU CAN USE TO FOCUS ON POSITVE SELF TALK RATHER THAN NEGATIVE SELF THINKING.

TEACHNIQUE NUMBER 1
THOUGHT FLIPPING.

When you realize that you are thinking negatively.

You should take a step back take a depth breath and think about how you can reword things to be more positive

HERE'S AN ACTIVITY FOR YOU THERE ARE NO RIGHT OR WRONG ANSWER

Let's say you started playing the guitar and you weren't good you might have thoughts like

'Why am I so bad at this'
'I hate playing the guitar this is rubbish'

What could you say to make this a more positive thought?

☺

?

HERE'S AN SOME EXAMPLES
✗
'Why am I so bad at this'

⬇ Thought flip

'Although I'm not good now i know with a bit of practice I will only get better'
✓

HERE'S ARE SOME EXAMPLES

✗

'I hate playing the guitar this is rubbish'

⬇ Thought flip

'I love a challenge, I'm going to work hard to make sure I get better'

✓

20

Thought flipping

Make you see things in a much more positive way. So the conversation in your head is always kind to you.

Thought flipping also means you change
I CAN'T
TO
I CAN I LOVE A CHALLENGE

POSITIVE SELFTALK

Positive self-talk helps you see the positive side of things when thing's aren't going your way. It's a great way to be positive when the fact the ups and downs of day to day life

TECHNIQUE NUMBER 2
SELF-TALK PROMOTERS

This includes surrounding yourself with the right people. Make sure your friends are positive.

Make sure you exercise and eat healthy meals. This is been proven to increase positive self-talk and emotions

TECHNIQUE NUMBER 3
PRACTIVE GRATOITUDE

Gratitude is simply being thankful for all the good things in your life. This is a way to divert your attention if you start thinking negatively.

Thank you!

You have now learned 3 simple techniques to help with your positive self-talk.

THOUGHT FLIPPING
SELF-TALK PROMOTERS
PRACTICE GRATOITUDE

BY TRAINING SELF-TALK, YOU WILL BECOME:

More in tune with your emotions.

You will be able to manage stress

You will become more resiliant

It takes:

Time

Practice

Patience

It will help you keep balanced and focuse.

YOU have the power to
achieve anything YOU want.

YOU just have to believe and
work hard.

Say these MAGICAL words out loud.

I am SPECIAL

I am CREATIVE

I am HARDWORKING

I am in FULL CONTROL of my life

Thank you!

Thank you so much for reading my book. I hope you enjoyed it and discover lots of new things.

Education is very important. So keep working hard and keep positive.

If you enjoyed this book LET mummy knows about the things you've learned.

Also, let mummy know to make sure to leave a positive review and to look out for more books by

Sammy Smith

Resource List

Wei, A. (2021). 8 Mindfulness Habits You Can Practice Everyday. Retrieved 18 January 2021, from https://shop.projecthappiness.org/blogs/project-happiness/8-mindfulness-habits-you-can-practice-everyday?gclid=CjwKCAiAgJWABhArEiwAmNVTB2a_A0B0RFRcwDA3FDF2PwBb46HqIIvERgWSonvX-0RQcpnWsTq_NBoC7WEQAvD_BwE

3 ways to talk yourself up. Retrieved 18 January 2021, from https://au.reachout.com/articles/3-ways-to-talk-yourself-up#:~:text=Positive%20self%2Dtalk%20makes%20you,looks%20on%20the%20bright%20side.&text=Negative%20self%2Dtalk%20tends%20to,recovery%20from%20mental%20health%20difficulties.

Cardiff, C. Affirmations I Benefits of affirmations I How to create I Examples of I Q & A. Retrieved 18 January 2021, from https://www.clinicalhypnotherapy-cardiff.co.uk/affirmations

Emmons, R. (2010). 10 Ways to Become More Grateful. Retrieved 18 January 2021, from https://greatergood.berkeley.edu/article/item/ten_ways_to_become_more_grateful1

Heartfulness UK - Find peace and joy in being yourself. (2021). Retrieved 18 January 2021, from https://www.heartfulness.uk/?utm_source=DIGITALNRG&utm_medium=cpc&utm_campaign=Mindfulness_GEO&gclid=CjwKCAiAgJWABhArEiwAmNVTB4iCDQadtS_m2pZSPGxvqXQtd6uQ23m0b0TVVWkhNdlyIaIS9E-KQRoCQ9IQAvD_BwE

Retrieved 18 January 2021, from https://www.tenterdenmindfulness.co.uk/?gclid=CjwKCAiAgJWABhArEiwAmNVTB878sZgg0-Pe36n8IJ3ujrTzLQvIImIDL8mx70xHPAIOLpUmtIHS2RoCMtoQAvD_BwE

J.Legg, T. (2020). Positive Self-Talk: Benefits and Techniques. Retrieved 18 January 2021, from https://www.healthline.com/health/positive-self-talk#benefits-of-self--talk

Jones, A. (2013). 34 Ways to Show Gratitude & Have a Better Life Instantly - How to Get Out of Debt Fast - And Then We Saved. Retrieved 18 January 2021, from https://andthenwesaved.com/34-ways-to-show-gratitude/

Positive Self-Talk. (2020). Retrieved 18 January 2021, from https://www.youtube.com/watch?v=7l_NkXgAKIg

What Is Mindfulness? I The Mindfulness Toolkit. (2018). Retrieved 18 January 2021, from https://www.youtube.com/watch?v=k0SI0p3IuiQ

Printed in Great Britain
by Amazon